AF597996

VANILLA CUSTARD

frontispiece Ah-shi-sle-pah, Chaco Canyon, New Mexico

vanilla custard

judith morgan alexander

FLOATING ISLAND PUBLICATIONS

POINT REYES STATION

1988

ISBN: 0-912449-23-3

Published by:
Floating Island Publications
P.O. Box 516
Point Reyes Station, California 94956

Some of these poems have appeared in:
Amorotica: New Erotic Poetry (Deep River Press, Long Beach, California, 1981); *Creative Arts* (Ventura College); *Floating Island I, Like Old Friends, On Our Backs, Syzygy* (Ventura College); *Urthkin, Woodstock Times, Venice Beachhead* and *The Ojai Valley News.*

vanilla custard first appeared in *Floating Island I* (1976) and has been reprinted in *Urthkin, Like Old Friends, Creative Arts* and *The Ojai Valley News.* It was performed in 1976 in a Women's International Year festival in New York City.

Prairie Shoes and *Start in the Sun* were performed by Joyce Suskind in Carnegie Recital Hall, 1 March 1986.

Special thanks for support and erudition to Joyce Suskind, Jim Reed, Norma Smith, Linda Macaluso, George Wymer, Stella Resnick, Alan Kishbaugh, Betty Dodson, Joan Halifax and, without question, the one and only Michael Sykes.

Cover by Colleen Kelley.
Musical notation by Music Publishing Services, New York, NY.

for my mother, Carlyn Kohn Alexander (1912–1983)
and her mother, Corinne Wineland Kohn (1889–1984)

Contents

Sacrifice of the Heart: a poem with photographs

Ojai

Start in the Sun

Prairie Shoes

CHORUS:

Rock to the sky of the end nod and drowse your

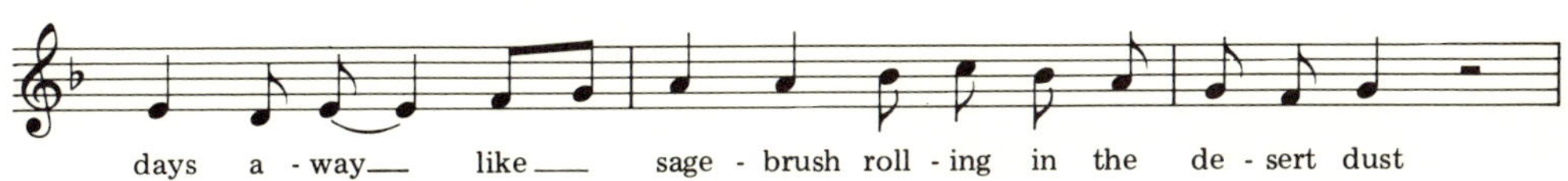

days a - way like sage - brush roll - ing in the de - sert dust

1.
2.
Rock to the sky of the end His And the hands cry

and the fac - es gaze and the

years e - rase the world and time turns days in - to

3
3
rock-ing chair dreams And there's no - where to go at all.

WOODSTOCK

bugle blue and holy domed
by trails and terraces
we feather the land
mapping past the long corrals
the eagled views
and nest among the hills.

and this is home
a migratory sighting place
a point of view
this autumn harvest
honey bees
the cider mills acrid
near the paper muddy puddles.

and we arrive
to stairs and fields
starry and warm
the birches ochring scarlet.

blood of the hills
we cut the cord once more
to wipe the corners
of the land.

and in the trace of sand
fingering time's edge
the shell crackling the waters
thinning and milky
i arrived

and without explanation
in that narrow hall
the floors caked
with waxen turtle skins
the hulls of old split ships
the moat dry as marrow

i imagined
that once
the dancers twirled here
efflorescent
to the strumming banjoes and fiddlers
the cards strewn now
in pillowed bundles
near the entrance.

under the eaves
there is a smoky smell
uneven and bony.

it is easy to choke.
i light the fire
and set
my self
aflame.

in the mirroring cotillion
a phoenix from ashen eden
in that final loneliness
glassy and echoing
wall upon wall upon wall

knotting eternity
i glow.

spoons and mallets
circle the tiers
clattering row upon row.
the feathers splinter halls
and entranceways.

i applaud the show.

a minstrel is ballooning
on my sleeve
and looking down
i see
grown to my arm
a small perfect self.

there's no escape
it says gnawing my bone.

i think to grimace
at the end
and smile.

i cherish you too much
to let you go
and crawls inside my elbow
unflapping the skin.

trust me.
disappearing.

in my spiral home
i twirl around
to know
i am
alone.

CARRIER TO ESALEN

*"Here are your waters and your watering place.
Drink and be whole again beyond confusion."*
–Robert Frost, *Directive*

bucketing the fog
the water carrier
patches in and out
of hills
to blanket the cool
voiceless sun

and drops confusion
tenderly
into the sea
salted in exactness

confusion and the sea are one
a constant illusion

the day burns mirrors into
windows

and i am a traveler
come to drink
at this watering place
a nourishing gap
timeless and wise

to this transparency
i carry my cup
and my bowl
emptying and
ready.

FLETCHER'S HOUSE

they tramp through the pantry
knocking over plates and cups
and hide behind the cellar door
giggling silly school girls
pigtailed pinafore

cross doorways stop to chat
and dancing singing late at night
across the lawn
pine-bedded thick
they arch to bolt
between the white oak and the ash
smooth bones turning open
under flesh as old as that

there's no one in the house you know
that's what the realtor said

and shadowed by the fire
on whiter walls reflected
bark to the lawn
they fade into the villa
empty for winter
too cold to cartwheel on the roof
and arabesque my window

i found a tile upon the grass
and looking up
to see a nick
a tile could not have fallen
from it's place
the others quite at home

the window near my ear cracks
i hear the knock
the click
again.

I've come to this house singing my own song
abandoning for months that slowing speed.
Love is so short. Forgetting is so long.

Above the yellowing birch I howl
in dark eclipse the hour of the moon
because I've come to this house singing my own song.

No one hears me cry. Not deer or dogs.
The pain and terror, terminals are cracked.
I'd love to forget the longing.

Winter starves the sparrows and the crow
their winging widens in my eye
because I've come to this house, slow.

It is not home for me, not yet
a passerby these mountains, traveling.
Love, forgetting is so long. I cry.

My palette is the sky. My thigh bone strong.
I paint myself on spangled stars.
I've come to this house singing my own song.
Love is so short. Forgetting is so long.

"seven broken watches one of them i fixed and wear
here's a pin she made yes and those oils on the wall
oh and that one in the other room the still life above
the mantle. she did that too. this was her jewish star,
from her mother."

Sally Siegel

counted time
wrote thank-you notes in
Coney Island Hospital
missed appointments
forgotten dinner dates
had cancer of the bone
and
didn't want to know.

Pray for the light
safe journey
where you travel.
We are one.

"i came home because i knew she was dying. i thought i could help her experience her own death. she wasn't interested."

Sally Siegel

came home to die
with her soft marrow and secrets

went into a coma
and
missed her own death.

Pray for the light
safe journey
where you travel.
We are one.

– Point Reyes Station
july 1976

from the New York Post, *October 1, 1975*

a sweet young thing from kansas
she met her man
the name of john g ball

lucky ball they called him
he swallowed swords by trade

and head over heels she fell in love
married him ran off to join the carnival

he said to her
'my estelline' twirling his moustache
'learn on the heavy blade
then you can swallow anything.'

and for a year
she practiced before breakfast
then they were billed as
lucky prince and princess estelline

one time dear estie
ate a bayonet
ram-jammed it down her throat
next day she didnt come to work
that anger internalized

and what could doctor do
heal the inside of a tunnel
rest drink juices bleed internally

now she and lucky are no more
her second hubbie died
her son sells tires in kansas
and swallows tire irons

a crazy way to earn your keep
'kept me from doin' a lot
of other things i didn't want to do.'

pinched her innards a while back
now she just swallows stove pokers

and lady estelline of hoxie ball
now's estelline of pike.

for Phil Ochs

1.

On Ninth Avenue
country goats
hang
upside down
stringing hooves
to spike limp tendons

head stuffed
in plastic
sweaty and breathless
bulging eyes
baby blue
opaque as Death

Where have you gone
my sweet
my little one

the skin peeled clean
drying by the door
leaves as ash-pink frame

Open air disguises the smell
of Death

THIS WEEK ONLY
SALE ON OX TAILS

blue grey tongues
dismembered
piled by kidneys hocks
and brains

Where have you gone
my sweet
my little one

2.

He's dead
said Leslie.
Hanged.
At his sister's

That death is mine
a certain ordering
of things
arrangements charts.

The phone is ringing.
No answer.

A year ago
you serenaded
me and Stella
Ohio minstrel
sang of Africa
and blew your nose

on Rock 'n Roll the seventh floor
Chelsea Hotel
elevator always broken
yellow high-heeled dude
glitter in the groin
hip city blues.

You have a halo round your head.

The war is over Phil.
It's over.

Where have you gone
my sweet
my little one

IT'S JUST ANOTHER ORDINARY BORING AUTUMN THURSDAY IN WOODSTOCK, STELLA

October 10: i arrived here yesterday. stop.
really arrived.
i've come to live
live here
stop.
love,

i sent myself that telegram

i've come to the mountains
to gather myself
to my center.
stop.
to be still.

where concerts of geese
flock winging to honk
their high position in the skies

cross crows to caw
leaves spiraling one after the other
to crimson orange lemon yellow
chestnut seal brown crack whip
jittery horse chill autumn
shake and twirl.

i went to the bus station in kingston
cackling to myself thinking
"i've taken you to airports in
denver boston monterey california
from big sur up the raggedy coast
through steep fog
and now
it's just a trailways station
in kingston new york."

"so it's come to this" peter said.

"welcome home"
i said to you.
home to the mountains.
to myself.
stop.
stop running.
be still at the center.

i went to watch you ride a horse
there you sat
astride a sweet little bay mare
posting no hands on a longe line
dressed like denmark in krumville.

we stopped along the road.
stop.
to watch a cow
nursing her young calf
picked a milk pod

you filled the gas tank
at the arco station

saw milking cows battle
hornless
one female mounting the other
to butt among the herd
their cuds hanging intentions.

"it's just another ordinary boring autumn thursday
in woodstock, stella," i said.

pale lace light between the maples
the palace in the woods
we didn't find
'estellina' built of stone
appearing out of no where.

i like to travel with you.
anywhere.
such beauty in your traveling.
grace.
you talked of trust
of opening more all the time
feeling secure

"it's the mountains" you said
"living with mountains.
i came here from boulder.
mountains. i love them.
ron asked me why
i moved around all the time.
i'm looking for a reason to stay still."

i heard you then
the sound resound
hollowing to bounce
against my bones my skull
leaves bark and sky

a silent opening lens
my senses were all cameras
slowing to stop.
slowing.   stop.
freeze frame.

and the mountains know peace
the window's eyes.

the mountains know too.
they are still.

VANILLA CUSTARD

once when i was very small i tasted vanilla custard it was the best custard i had ever eaten and enid and her father myron and i went to willow grove park and he took us on the roller coaster and i wore a yellow sunsuit with blue ducks on it and i dribbled the custard all over myself that was half the fun and i loved enid's father and one spring during the war he built a fence around their house all by himself and he bought me a big vanilla custard and he killed himself the summer i was ten i was away at camp and my parents didnt tell me until i got home late in august he died at the age of thirty three and i cried for a long time and i was angry at my parents for hiding the truth from me. i did understand. death is for children too.

and i still think of enid she's the first person i can remember knowing and now i cant find her and i still look for the vanilla custard it would really be a lie to say i'd given up the notion of ever finding it in fact i look all the time whenever i go to an amusement park or smell a certain smell or recognize a face reminiscent of that place way back there once upon a time in my footed pajamas where every smell was soap and every taste vanilla custard and i dont tell anyone that's what i'm looking for only i know and now you know that i look in chocolate eclairs and rice pudding and cup custard and frozen custard and flan and bavarian cream filled donuts and boston cream pie and french vanilla ice cream and tapioca pudding and i cant let go of it.

and i know i'm lying to myself i wouldn't recognize it if i did find it it was so long ago i cant even be sure now it ever really happened and still i keep looking i keep looking it's not even the custard anymore it's just something something else i lost when i was four.

manhattan
january 1975

VENICE

for Stuart Z. Perkoff

I lived in your house
on Horizon sometime
after your death
and though we never met
your comfort/able spirit
words and murmurs
always held my middle-of-the-night
awakening wolves

"The opposite of profound is silly."
– Carl Jung

Sing to me, song to me
running to run
canoe to the moon
to the sun, to the sun

Paddle me, puddle
my porridge is cold
we grow younger each year
we grow old, we grow old

At the Saint Vincent de Paul Thrift store
    in San Rafael
between the lampshades and the
    used mattresses
I found one children's canoe paddle
    among a cannister of crutches

Nobody is going to call me a cripple

Lake Paradox: 1948

At the age of nine
rising to my chin
I learned to paddle
soft in the water
dipping quiet as Indians
and
pared my toenails
waiting for the arrival of
my Prince Charming

Now I just hang around
waiting for myself

How can I find me
where am I today
in this courtyard of dreams
where the sky's made of clay

sand in my shoes
running to run
canoe to the moon
to the sun, to the sun

It is a dream of children
an unredeemable stamp
a marginal reminder
a button

I do not deliver mail
I do not burden myself with the
change of season
I do not burden myself with items
except
when waiting is required
except
when they bear great
symbolic significance
except
when they turn color
are made of bone
cannot be eaten whole
require soaking
need careful laundering
collect no interest
except
when there are exceptions

Paddling to the Great Pyramid
I often go up stream
backwards
with nothing but a tea strainer

Sing to me, song to me
running to run
canoe to the moon
to the sun, to the sun

Paddle me, puddle
my porridge is cold
we grow younger each year
we grow old, we grow old

Hannah Fleisher
a nice Jewish princess
running backwards and forwards
a palindromatic madam oh no
perspiring
up and down in the ladies locker room
flashing her racquet
and her can of Spalding balls
Hannah bumping into things
her armpits stink two broken nails
Hannah her hair
falling in her face
Hannah a silly banana
she was her own fool

Hannah Fleisher
she was a dreamer
a plotter of plays rehearsing her life
grew up with cashmeres and country club manners
didnt mark the liquor bottles ate with the help
saw people who hadnt and noticed the difference

Hannah left home in search of her madness
her Jewish prince charming a frog
and hardly a doctor

Hannah never dreamed of station wagons
railroad platforms Hadassah and 2½ children

She dreamed of adventure
of indians on horseback thin mist
rising in the desert the death
of moonlight her freedom

and when i grow up shed say
im gonna run away from home
im gonna do what I wanna do
nobodies gonna tell me
i wont have to clean my plate if i dont want to
i dont care if the children in Asia are starving
im gonna say what i wanna say
feel what i wanna feel
love whoever i love nobodies
gonna tell me

Hannah Fleisher
a nice Jewish princess
ran from the manners
lay plates and laundresses
Hannah wanted her freedom more than
anything else in the whole wide world

and as the old saying goes
theres no stopping a jewish indian princess

Hannah Hannah no silly banana

freedoms too ripe for peeling
she says
and licks her plate clean

kneeling in the field
one last piece of freedom
remaining Venice I dont go home

    home in Venice sliced thin
    i am a charlie sandwich
    one on each side
    Royal palm on lettuce hold the mayo home

backyard peach cemetery
sticks to my birkenstocks
flies on fruity corpses
buzzing up the courts up figs
and babcocks home

Ophelia would have wished for such another death
soft afternoon skin sweet stench of light
delicious death swollen delivered rotten fruit
no matter
earth to earth she is received.

I dont go home.
Instead I go to the laundramat.
I only think I need to go home

    back street pipe dream
    ivory blonde long-legged suntan roller skater
    sweet whore Venice home

I buy two extra boxes of All for the sheets and towels.
I want them really clean.
I think to take an enema when I get home.

    how i lay me down to sleep
    i pray the Lord my soul to keep waking
    hair falling long on the pillow

home to vague
photos browning at the edges
Atlantic City toast and jam
my mother's open-toed alligator pumps
four-no-trump to jitterbug the Boardwalk
I Do Not Live In Marvin Gardens
purple toenails lips and sand

behind the laundramat
hilly illusion of Everest
two steps and I'm up. I sit down.

traffic going nowhere but home
you'd think passing by
it's just another empty topsoil/dumphill/ten foot high LOT
hot steal at four mil
LA smoothie tight white disco suit gold chain
white shoes cigar white Lamborghini
buy it up quick profit home

wild the grasses plantain chicory home grown Venice
yellow daisies empires of ants
isnt anyone going to tell them it's time to move home
close that one Joe/it's over fill the hole

rich brown virgin/flat/good for farming soil
spoons and safety pins are bones of these dead
caterpillar claws mark the grey soul
simple as forgotten weeds i weep

and it's not really anything this field
a certain way the light falls
a shadow an unexpected turn in the road
a voice remembered a dream

this is no dream Laertes
my bones, the bones of these dead
a place to lay me down home

I'm tired.
I dont want to go anywhere else.
not now.
Home's the best place to be Toto.

kneeling in the field
one last piece of freedom
remaining Venice I dont go home. home.   I am home.

I fold the towels first.

Venice, California
17 august 1978

he found a button in
his coffee Häagen-Dazs

soft
who rubbed her
orlon breasts
up against the cold
vat dripping that
second time she wore
her sweater

hard already little
balls around her brown
nipples wet dripping
taffy berry creme
between her legs

she spoons her mother-
of-pearl
into his mouth

and i take my fingers the first two
stick them in my mouth licking them wet
then i put them in your mouth opening you inside
and i put my fingers slowly into your wetness waiting
watching you start to settle spin slowly against them
rocking your bones moaning
my tongue inside you wet

you
lying there your eyes
dreamoanmoving from one elbow to the other
jolt you stop stop
bolt suddenly into my arms
heat of your legs
im coming filling you im coming you scream
not yet

not yet its like riding the IRT between cars
letting the vibrations of the train run up my legs
not yet
into my cunt feeling the rails not yet clacking
the tracks air blows up
my pants not yeT closing my eyes my tongue
into you not yet nOW you scream
i cant wait   im coming NOT YET right here
yes baby im coming wet youre so wet NOW im coming
now just as the train pulls into the station

now

Here comes ENneYday Feeney   click clickety click click

patten leather mary janes pink pinafore
cute as a button and
ENneYday

"Hi ya, hi ya hot tomato
whatcha' doin' hunney bunney"

"Whatcha got in mind ENneYday
You hot?"

Second Hand Rose sucked her thumb. All her life she sucked her thumb and she sucked lemons and hot soup and cocks. She sucked nipples and she sucked pacifiers. She didnt get to suck her Mama's breast so she was catchin' up.

ENneYday she came up close as she could to Second Hand Rose who she loved with a passion.

"Rose my sweet, my Rose, my darlin'
hot tomato hunney bunney are you hot?"

"Asked you first ENneYday."

Now she said yes and they did/fall/slow as the ground/
would let them fall/down into each other's arms/right
there in the street.

The passion took them and ENneYday made sweet moaning sounds and Second Hand Rose opened herself right there with the dogs and the cats and the children watching/
rolled around gripping each other like horses/ENneYday
and Rose.

Can we just leave them there in the street making love?

WHY NOT??

As Homer says begin to begin *en medias res* pick up anywhere and end anywhere because we know it just goes on anyway, right ENneYday?

She smiles. Another secret smile. The best writing I think is a secret to yourself.

I went to a journal writing workshop. The teacher was talking about writing secrets to yourself as one of the keys to the journal. She suggested each of us write a secret on a piece of paper. Then she would read them out loud so we could get an idea of what other people thought were secrets.

I sat there with my piece of paper. I couldn't think of a good secret. Suddenly, I looked around the room and noticed this absolutely gorgeous woman sitting in the corner and of all the people there, she was the one who caught my eye.

And I felt hot. So I wrote:

The woman in the corner makes me hot.

Even I didnt know that until I wrote it down.

She read the secrets. One person said, "I get depressed alot." One said "I get angry with my wife and I don't tell her." Things like that.

She read my secret last. My heart was pounding in my mouth and I thought she wasn't going to read it at all. She opened the paper slowly, read it to her self, gulped and then went on:

The woman in the corner makes me hot.

It got a good laugh. I imagined that all the men in the room were wondering which one of them wrote it and that all the women were wondering about the woman in the corner.

I kind of wanted to stand up and say, "Hey! I wrote that" but then it wouldn't have been a secret anymore.

"Are you hot enough, ENneYday?"

"Rose, are you hot?"

Is that a secret?/ STOP.

and their world stopped/stopped right there for them/
right there in the street/ when time became only sensation/
and the sound/ moanings/ the blend of two spirits/
simply /
union into the one.

1. Allegro

soft in my ear breath
beat at your throat

cunt soft sun
tongue deep in my
mouth

we speak only in cadences
authentic repose

mute fingers hammer into
action dark boxes
arranged to play
a piacere
with pleasure only
we are such instruments

Mozart alone
edging towards harmony
dark room lightening
sun coming up cunt sun

kissing his music
allegro con moto
his fingers flicker
the keys licks
his lips cunt sun

soft in my ear breath
beat at your throat

tongue coming up
warm in my mouth
in your cunt

like symphonies

2. Largo

still sweet still
dark across the lake

touch me your mouth
stroke/feather/stroke

still still
in darkness
leave as we travel
such thin strips of
wisdom dip
return

dark as the lake dark
eyes still your gaze

in stillness we travel
quiet we paddle

alone

3. Scherzo

she comes she calls
i dream i pray

we are a wide river

come bright heart
come cross the
soul of my
tongue of my
touch of my
gypsy my lover

and the light drifting yellow water always
delivers the night

4. Rondo

falling
we are always
falling falling
into time in time
through through time

and passing

falling and passing
passing each other and passing
passing each other and falling

out sounds silent
falling and passing
echo into the meadow's wedge
dark trees in the dusk dogs
bark far away out sounds
falling and passing

nod your head yes nod
your eyes yes
nesting
there are feathers in your mouth
you rest

rest your head and sleep
lay beside me little child
and by and by we'll rise
falling and passing
touching each other in the dark
licking and sucking and stroking and eating
and crying and moaning and fucking and falling

and falling and passing

nothing changes
i got what i wanted that was all
everything else is exactly the same

falling
falling and passing
falling
falling and falling

and rising

Will the Congregation please rise
and turn to page 531, Psalm 23

singer my sweet
she went away she told me to pretend she was going out of town
The Lord is My Shepherd
I Shall not Want
that wasn't true i knew that
i'd drive by her house see her car out front
her lights were on i knew she was home
playing her saxophone on the back porch
she'd turn on the answering machine and screen her calls
but she told me to pretend she was out of town
that she went away

she didnt call or
come to the window knocking anymore
at six in the morning
singer she made up excuses and told lies
to cover up things she didnt want me to know about

she went away my hands
numb from the pain her
leaving without saying hardly anything
hot not wanting to let go
like holding
cold metal jacks and a jack ball at recess
and no one to play with
golf ball skin thickened for hitting
and when it slit you could slip the skin off
peel all the bands
thousands of little strands all stuck together
to get to that hard core in the middle
bounce high as the sky
ups and downs cherry in the basket

my fancy she went away
rocket to the moon her eyes told me secrets
she carried in her pockets
timing her visits
together by clocks
she has so much to say she's mute
so she went away instead
She maketh me to lie down in green pastures
She leadeth me beside the still waters
She restoreth my soul
I didnt notice at first
it was so hard to get it through my head
that she went away
as if she had never been there at all
except i knew she had
i could feel her still

still she came
as sudden as she went away
standing there her lower lip
swollen and purply from
blowing reed sucking mother fucker
i'd like to sock her teeth down her throat
She leadeth me in the paths of righteousness
for Her name's Sake
left me standing there
ran from my insistence
right into the hot spot
white as sound she didnt know
quite where to stand the stage
filling with lights climbed there
her knees bleed that was what she wanted
she went away
she told me to pretend she was out of town
she kept saying that
and i had a hard time hearing her

and when she really went
alone i held myself
in her imaginary arms
and i know her leaving
had nothing to do with me at all

and so

I am Keeping Still, the Mountain
Nine in the third place
Keeping Still the hips the sacrum
stiff. Dangerous. The heart suffocates.

She Went Away and I am Keeping Still.

all i said was
pretend im out of town im here
but its hard to reach me
its hard to reach you i say reaching
my arms open wide to you she went away
reaching back to me her arms
skittery and scared running at the slightest
singer my sweet out
to the stars this week in her reaching
she didnt go away she's just out of town
singing my hands beside the still waters
Yea though I walk
through the Valley of the Shadow of Death
she didnt go away
i can tell myself the truth now
I will fear no evil for Thou Art with me
Perfect Love casteth out fear she told me
i love you remember that

And she went, quietly, singing, away

ROOMS EMPTYING

for Robert Irwin

i.

she emptied the closets threw away
the old magazines and rags
and when she put the last trash out
in the alley

there was nothing in the room
at all

then
she took off the front
of her
store for him

he painted everything white
white as the light as the skylight white
as the sky
as the room
still silent

he wanted a blank page on Market Street
bright skin across the fourth wall
right up to the edge of the sidewalk

so he stapled the sky to the ground
containing the emptiness

only
it slipped through the fabric
out
oozing to the beach to cover everything
the emptying room filling with light

spirits of wind
spirits of space

vibrating pulsing now

still as the silence

and emptying

ii.

when her heart split in two
she emptied her days
and her shoes
they almost killed her

only the room can contain now
her vulnerable solitude
only her emptiness filling again
only her body releasing desire
song of her soul
lay me down to rest
this weary traveler
some days she cannot stand up

only her nest in the cradle
of God
frail bird bright wing
ah she is an emptying angel

iii.

they brought cameras
took pictures of nothing
pictures of white and the silence
emptiness shifting as the wind shifts
drifting down Market Street
out free on Speedway
spreading shadows
past the palm lawn to the sea

then she put
the front back
on the building

now there was nothing
containing the emptiness
no smudges on the door sill
no Chevy stationwagon
parked all night right
in front

such a frail entrance
too tight for intruders
him with his broom every morning
sweeping the unbroken membrane

white as the light
spirits of wind
spirits of space
still as the silence
and emptying

make room for me room
i am an empty cup filling
and she is an emptying angel
and he painted everything
white as the light
as the emptying room
removing illusion

1.

only so close
she came apart at the seams
screaming

thin rocker drumming
he practiced patience

one last night
in the parking lot at Merlin's
packing his high hat

dont help me
i need the practice
                    practice
                    practice your drums man
                    practice cooking
                    practice doing the laundry
                    practice cleaning the toilet
                    solo
                    practice having a backache
                    practice protection

                    practice answering the phone
                    practice staying up all night
                    mixing chinese herbs
                    practice prayer and silence
                    giving up desire
                    practice patience

it takes so long
couple years ago i'd a left
now i lay me down to sleep
i pray the Lord
keep breathin' baby
give it up desire aint worth it
not this time not yet Lord

this middle-of-the-night Death
almost blew her brains out
aint her time not Raggedy Anne
sock wobbly legs her husky vocals
still she's got those
angel blues to sing

2.

died she almost died
from the music business
almost got her down
on her knees she's
bleeding
it aint got to rock her soul
the music just aint cant you write
some disco honey
shake his fat hand smile sucker
sign right here ya' start tomorrow

died she almost died

3.

The club is dark.
It's three thirty in the morning.
They'd a' packed up the truck
for the five thousandth time.
She'd still be buzzing
from blowing her
brains out like eggs
blue lights flashing behind
her eyes.

after airlessendlesshours of
playingsweatingsingingcoughingsippingstopping   playingsweating
breathe the throat smoky alcoholic stink of nicotine

bouncer cracking drunk skull
ripe watermelon slammed on the sidewalk
you leafshaking in the streetscared
too many women in the crowded bathroom
no place to go justtobe

alone

i need to be alone more when i go away for oneday its not enough
i want so much

samsara

alone

alone in the still silence

thickdistancesoftrees

so simple an island

and the

river passing by

After the loud neighbor rock n' roll
squealing tires of teenage muggers
gunshot screams in the rapeback alley

weekend carnival/commotion of tee shirts/
fruit vendors/fruits/cyclists/skaters/
swimmers/artists/lost towels and children/
mommies pushing strollers/daddies/dollies/dogs/
dropped ice cream cones/cotton candy/drunks and bikers/
pinball machines/congas/pickpockets/jugglers/
umbrellas/skateboards/kites/strolling players/

street musicians/rich white folks from beverly hills
looking for something they won't find
honkies/oakies/hippies/tourists/
pimps and whores

broken mirror balloons how you
begin to see yourself

                    and the Poor.

We are all the little children of God.

Lay me down to rest
by the reed wide river
this weary traveler her nest
in the cradle of God.

After the prayer and the meditation
after the fasting and the purification

        silence and union

after the dying of the blue light
after Death
          playing her saxophone
puts away her case and contract
ball point pen

SHE AINT SIGNIN' THAT ONE.

No. We looked over the contract.
Not this time.
          NOT THIS TIME I SAID.

Ya' hear me.   Ya' hear me, Death.

She aint signin' this time.

Yes.   Yes.   God   still
                    still

she gots to be a singin' /   praise God /   yes

still

she gots to get up on her own two feets agin/   un huh/

still

taps her feets
clip clicks her tongue
wiggles her fingers

still

she gots to practice her piano

Yes God I knows it. yes

suck her reeds blow
herself slow as she can
into something she cannot know about.

Yes.

she gots to be singin' somewhere

I knows it yes I do.

cause I can hear her

singin'

still

yes, Hallelujah

singin' inside

Praise God

Hallelujah.

inside.

me.

Venice
August 1980

SACRIFICE OF THE HEART

mind of jaguar bleeds
torn open only
reversing the secrets

mind of jaguar moves
in death circles
sidestepping all danger

shadow bending into light
whitens clues of fear

mind of jaguar cups the clear
code and untraceable
water

Uxmal, Yucatan
22 January 1986

Temple of Kukulcan: Chichen Itza

Jaguar with shoes: Valladolid

House of the Dovecote: Uxmal

Palapa roof: Chac Mool (Tulum)

Mayapan

Carnival car: Valladolid

The Nunnery: Uxmal

Papaya tree: Uxmal

Fisherman's temple: near Xel-ha

Palapa: Chac Mool (Tulum)

EN ESTA CASA NACIO EL 2 DE ABRIL DE 1833,
EL SEÑOR GENERAL DON
FRANCISCO CANTÓN.
2 DE ABRIL DE 1933

Valladolid

At the eye doctor in Dzitas

Ceremony for vision quest: Ah-shi-sle-pah near Nageezi, New Mexico

Door with hat: Valladolid

Canyonlands, Utah

OJAI

Absent sun turns mountains blue. turns
shadow thin the skin already
trees to calligraphy
turns meeting to deliverance.

Spirit arrives.
On Her white horse.
I wake to Her presence.
Blood to blood communion
it's a perfect rendezvous.

Only the counterpoint of crickets
and distant dogs
echo the endless
and sacred beating
of the One Compassionate Heart.

I turn turn because it is time
because what She is is turning
because if I don't turn
some corner, inclination
habit of the heart
there will be no more turning.

And so I turn.

A great peace descends beyond name.
It is the ordinary sound of God breathing
the way She turns without moving.

lokaya: Chumash Indian word for stillness

thicketsofweeds c g
r n
i i
s
s s P
o U
r Y
c a
w

high

into the

s w o l l e n gorge

deep slit

deathswooning palms
fanswarm this wet cemetery
down on their knees
to the still trickle of their teacher.

The trees pray. In stillness. Lokaya.

The trees pray in stillness down on their knees
beside the healing waters.

O, the Water
Lokaya, the Stillness
Holy Sound of Spirit Round
Fall we are Lifted.
We are come to be healed.

The trees pray.

Pray to the Spirit of Smoke and Rain
Pray to the Spirit of Stillness. Lokaya.
Pray to the Spirit of the Warm Healing
        Sulphur Water holy spirit passing
        through my skin rotten egg soda
        swallowcleansing

Water water babies
drinking chromium bicarbonate
fall we are lifted
we are come to be healed.

earthspirittreespiritwaterspirit one.

I couldnt raise my leg another inch.
Ripdeep palm frond open red slits in my arms.
HEADLINE: Wounded Tree Lopper Comes to Healing Waters.

Come as the trees came
wounded skin slit open oozing sap
sounds of the dying blood shed curses
Matilija seering yahoos him
standing there coughingkickingspitting
on the land and dying.

The trees pray. In stillness.

For the angry wounded desecration of the land
for the broken promise violent barkshouting
clumsy stumbling fast talk ripoffs
in the basement

for the darkening of the Light.

I lean. Lean on the Spirit of Stillness.
Fall. I fall on my knees and listen.
Led. I am led beside the still waters.
Open. I stand before the empty gate
and am filled.

Wheeler Hot Springs
13 March 1981

stubborn as bone
they huddle at their chill bivouac
old haggy cacklers coyote crones
down from the hilly thrones of Topa Topa

at every moondog midnight
they make their awesome squalking racket
then run cunning to rile up
the coonhounds and steal their women.

They know their time
and their assignment.
It is God's law.

They bark the unutterable yappings.
Dog/God. Yahweh. Jehovah-Jireh.
Abba Father they wake me in the night, providing.

Signals of the moon
across the wide canyon
their wild screamings
rattle my tongue
the tongue of angels
cha bah wha noonah
eets da mahnoucha
kiko manna nokka
behballalocha

Dog yappings. God mutterings.
I lift my hands and murmur to the mountain.
Howbeit in the Spirit He speaketh mysteries.

Words flow from my mouth
like water and love without end
strange senseless words
words without ordinary meaning
unpronounceable undefinable unexplainable
words I recognize only in the heart
barbarian mutterings to God

No matter.
This intimate ignorance
is my utterance of praise.

Climbing the caduceus
                                        where no stumbling occurs
an arrow aimed at Heaven
                                        I knock upon each stair
step by narrow step
I mumble
                                        see see Lord that eye of surrender
                                                    that willing deliverance
                                                    that singing of a new song
step by narrow step
I pray
                                        humble in the presence of your love Lord
step by narrow step
I doven
                                        rocking to remember
                                        obedient coming again and again
up
                                        to the edge
and o p e n i n g .

I know my time and my assignment.
It is God's law.

I lift my hands and murmur.
Dog yappings.   God mutterings.

I speak the tongue of coyote
the tongue of angels.
The holy mountain has receiving arms.

Sisar Canyon
January 1982

for Denise Brennan, died 28 April 1981

you never aint even done got
threw high scool never
got past that

CHAINSTRUNGDARKACROSSFROMONE L O O S E LEDGETOTHEOTHER

no loitering bridge/ bud can empties/ STOP HERE

never knew neckfast what

HIT (snap) you.

Just quiet. Done. No Blame.

Our Father Who Art in Heaven
is this the amorous legend
is this what I was waiting for
a forgotten face in the yearbook.

Angelchild choking
back blood the Gentle
Spirits held your
soft head in passage.

Hey kid, I aint got the numbers
the magic.
Why? Because.
The answer is the question.

Just quiet. Done. No Blame.

RADIO GIRL

for Bobb Lynes

"Look, Tootsie, according to the Magee theory of Radio Dyanetics which I'm the guy that made it up, I claim that when you hear a broadcast once, it don't just disappear. You see, it's still out there. I mean, old radio programs never die. They're still out there, bouncin' around in the air, waitin' for somebody to tune 'em in again."

– Fibber Magee

Yes Molly they do do
bounce still out there

no no dont Fibber
open that closet
no Fibber dont

bounce on the airwaves
tuning my dial to Palmolive.

Star-struck myself a Mary Noble
third grade heartthrob
waiting for my backstage Larry
the stink of hot bananas and wee-wee
still in my cloakroom nostrils
I'd dash home
to the not-to-be-missed
always answers in the agony
Monday thru Friday
Life Can Be Beautiful. Could. It was.
I knew it in my heart of hearts.
I'd gunnite the drama to the popcorn.

I used to to think there were little people
stuffed inside the radio
and when the tubes were cool
I'd always pull away the back to check.

Moon over Stella Dallas
can a girl from a little mining town in Colorado
find happiness with a noble English lord?
Can she lurk with Lamont in the shadows
nightride in the Black Beauty
and hear the thundering hoofbeats of the great horse Silver
pulsing in her veins?
Can a girl BE Clark Kent and live to tell about it?

I ate my Ranger Joe and brushed with Ipana
cross my heart double bubble.
Radio Girl perfume was still 10 cents at Woolworths.
Everyone on Foxcroft Road sent away boxtops
for a Jack Armstrong pedometer and a decoder ring.
Everyone I knew wanted to be invisible.

Matilija Canyon
September 1984

buffing the nails to crochet
muzak is clean towels

chew jaw the chicle
PoP jawjaw poPpoP
chewjaw pop cheW

push the stroller into the trashcan

TIDEEASHWASHEASY (giggle mommie)

bYe (pop) sLAM

rollrollaround bounce
bounce on de groundroll

(buffing the nails)

bags and bags and bags of pillowcases stuffed
stinkysock stains greasy towels mudblood underwear

WE PICK UP AND DELIVER Same Day Clean

(buffing the nails)

MOre KIDs comethey SHouT and gigglegigglegiggle

jawjaw the chew (poP)
chicchicK the chicle

HIbYe sLAM (pop)

polish the car how this came cleaning
rags old rags

EZYWASHEZYDRY

s-s-s- StU CK whomPPPwhomp S T U C K ss . . t o p

(jaw) cHewjAw SNAP!!!

Everyonelooking

spill Dr. Pepper in washer number 17

still buffing her nails
twenty five minutes

I (JaW) fold . . chic . . (pop) . . . . BYE
quick towels mommie

CASEY'S GRACE

for my mother
Carlyn Dorothy Kohn Alexander
August 30, 1912–April 6, 1983

the nature is shift.
insistence of water.
flames madness wind
slipping through willow.

shift and slip.
only to be lifted.
in the living room chair.   Shift.
Stock quotations on the floor
and the ball scores.
Her bid. *Four hearts.*
Shift deeper.
Five no trump.
She slipped away
into her last shadowy darkness.
pass pass   *pass.*

In her satin dress
and thin-lipped red lipstick
I touched her finally beauty.
Stiff.
An uncertain shift in the dark box.
I held my death by my son's arm.

It drizzled at the cemetery.
Her perfection of shift.

She was lifted into her golden room.

on her birthday,
August 30, 1984

PHOTO BY SUZANNE ARMS

I was born with two teeth on March 10, 1939 in Philadelphia, daughter of Casey and Ernie Alexander. 1961: B.A., English, 1963: M.A., Theater, both from the University of Michigan. 1964: I made my Broadway debut as a chair in Brecht's *The Caucasian Chalk Circle* at The Repertory Theater of Lincoln Center. 1967: 1st teacher training in U.S., The Alexander Technique. Taught at Harvard, Columbia, NYU and The New School. 1977: Studied Postural Integration with Jack Painter and taught deep tissue work in southern California for 7 years. Gave it all uP for photography and study with Oliver Gagliani. I have one son, Christopher, and live in Ojai, California.

Designed and produced in the summer of 1987 by
Michael Sykes and Linda Jane Ray at Archetype West
in Point Reyes Station, California.
Printed and bound in an edition of 1000 copies in the winter of 1988
by McNaughton & Gunn, Inc., Ann Arbor, Michigan.
The type face is Galliard
and was set on an Editwriter 7500.
The cover drawing is by Colleen Kelley.

Other Titles from Floating Island Publications

Peter Wild, *Barn Fires*
32 pp, perfectbound, $3.00
Frank Graziano, *Desemboque*
48 pp, perfectbound, $4.00
Christine Zawadiwsky, *Sleeping With The Enemy*
32 pp, perfectbound, $4.00
Jeffery Beam, *The Golden Legend*
48 pp, perfectbound, $5.00
David Hilton, *Penguins*
24 pp, hand-sewn, $3.00
Joanne Kyger, *Up My Coast*
24 pp, hand-sewn, $3.00
Frank Stewart, *The Open Water*
64 pp, perfectbound, $5.00
Arthur Sze, *Dazzled*
60 pp, perfectbound, $5.00
John Brandi, *The Cowboy from Phantom Banks*
80 pp, smythe-sewn, $6.95
Peter Wild, *The Light on Little Mormon Lake*
32 pp, hand-sewn, $4.00
Kirk Robertson, *Two Weeks Off*
48 pp, hand-sewn, $5.00
Norbert Krapf, *Circus Songs*
32 pp, hand-sewn, $4.00
Cole Swensen, *It's Alive She Says*
88 pp, smythe-sewn, $5.00
Joan Wolf, *The Divided Sphere*
96 pp, smythe-sewn, $5.00
Eugene Lesser, *Drug Abuse in Marin County*
136 pp, smythe-sewn, $8.95
Adele Langendorf, *Denial*
64 pp, smythe-sewn, $5.00
William Witherup, *Black Ash, Orange Fire*
224 pp, smythe-sewn, $10.00
Frank Stewart, *Flying the Red Eye*
56 pp, smythe-sewn, $8.00

Floating Island I
120 pp, smythe-sewn, $6.95
Floating Island II
184 pp, perfectbound, $8.95
Floating Island III
160 pp, perfectbound, $12.95